TEEN
OF
INSANITY

Raising Your Teenager Without Raising Your Blood Pressure

by Sherrie Weaver

0 43422 69548 5

Cover Illustration by Market Force, Burr Ridge, IL
Typography by Roy Honegger

Published by Great Quotations Publishing Co.,
Glendale Heights, IL

Library of Congress Catalog Card Number: 95-81331

ISBN 1-56245-228-2

Printed in Hong Kong

This book is dedicated to Jessica, my own personal reference source on teenagers, and to Seth, who will be a teenager long before I'm ready for it.

Thanks and love to Daniel, without whom Jessica and Seth would not be, and thanks to Nancy, Alena, Leroy, Grace Mary and Tracie Marie.

Special Technical Consultant: Mom Weaver, who raised several teenagers of her own, including the one I married.

Age of Insanity

Like any other parent of teenage children, I have many questions. ('Why me, God?' comes to mind frequently.) There are many books available to help the parents of adolescents, and not all of them contain hemlock recipes. But none of the books on the market are written by someone who actually has teenage kids. Most of them say things like, "Explain to your child that his behavior is distressing to you and is having a negative effect on your home life, and he will no doubt cease the undesirable behaviors." This is the largest load of fertilizer I have ever sniffed. Teenagers don't give rat spit about how they are affecting home life. Most of them do not ever spend enough time out of their rooms to realize that there is more to the house than the kitchen, bathroom and telephone.

With this in mind, I've decided to write my own guide for parenting teenagers. The theory is that I can't possibly screw it up anymore than the educated professionals have, and with adolescents, who's going to notice, anyway?

Let's start with an easy question:

Q.-1. Is it permissible to put your teenage daughter in full-body restraints if she insists on trying out for cheerleading?

A. Yes. It's actually even desirable. Because during the entire try-out period, which can last up to 10 days in some schools, she will be bouncing around the house, making large, uncontrolled motions with her hands and feet and shouting little bits of non-sequiturs like 'Be Aggressive' and 'Slam Attack'. She will also be attempting to do cartwheels and round-offs, which will result in lots of time at the emergency room while highly paid medical professionals try to make her leg point straight again.

Q.-2 A carload of teenagers leaves Houston at 9 am traveling 50 mph. At that rate, how long before they're all hungry?

A I really hate math teachers. This is a trick question, because not only will you never find a carload of teenagers content to drive 50 mph, there's also no way they'd be on the road before noon.

Q.-3 Should you limit the amount of time a teenager can spend on the telephone?

A. You'll have to. Without some kind of restraint system in place, a teenager will spend so much time on the telephone that it will attach itself to her ear, and the surgery necessary to free her will not be covered by most insurances, which means you'll have to give up your Lake Powell vacation.

Q.-4 I have noticed that my teenage child is very moody and generally has a sullen attitude. Is this normal? If so, when can I expect it to stop?

A. All teenagers have a sullen attitude. It is what they are best at doing, and they go with their strengths. You can expect it to begin diminishing just about the time they are forced to make their first rent payment and do their own laundry. Then they will start being nice to you again, because they want to borrow money.

 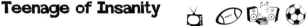

Q.-5 My teenager spends so much time with friends that I do not see him for days on end. How can I be sure he still lives here and has not run off to join the Peace Corps?

A. Leave a bottle of soda in the fridge, a box of breakfast pastries on the table and a plate of fried chicken in the microwave overnight. If, the next morning, you find only decimated containers and greasy fingerprints, you know that your teenager is around somewhere. Or leave a $20 bill (if you still have one) by the telephone, and if it disappears while you are folding laundry, your teenager is just fine.
Don't worry about him joining the Peace Corps. The Peace Corps will not let him sleep until noon and will expect him to do something constructive, which makes the whole deal unattractive. Plus, there is rarely a telephone anywhere the Peace Corps goes.

Q.-6 Sometimes I think my adolescent fakes an illness to get out of school. How can I tell if my teenager is really sick?

A Easy. Adolescents, like badgers, are denning animals. They will hole up in a dark cave and eat until someone drags them out. So, to tell if your kid is really sick, tap on their door with the telephone in your hand. Say something like, "Mr. Perfect-This-Week is on the phone. He wants you to meet him at the pizza joint in 15 minutes. What shall I tell him?" If the teenager in question shoots out of her room like a Congressman after a pay hike, you can bet she was feigning illness. If she doesn't move and instead says something like, "Nah, I'll just hang out here and read," call 911 immediately.

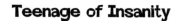 

Q.-7 My teenager dresses like she collided with a homeless person's cart outside a thrift store. Why can't she dress more normally?

A. Normally? You mean like high-waisted polyester pants, silk shirts and platform shoes with goldfish in the heels? I have a photo of myself in a kerchief cornered red polyester dress with silver spangles. My hair is pulled back with leather barrettes, there is a mood ring on my finger and my shoes are so high that when I took them off I had to decompress or risk the bends. At least your teenager is dressed, which is much better than certain modern rock bands who perform wearing a surgical mask and a guitar. There is no way a teenage boy can be looking at a teenage girl's caboose if she is wearing jeans loose enough for her father after Thanksgiving dinner and a plaid flannel shirt over a grey sweatshirt. Be glad they dress that way.

Q.-8 In this world of violence, rampant sexual perversion and Mighty Morphin Power Ranger dolls, is there any way a parent can raise a happy, well-adjusted, polite, respectful child?

A No. But maybe you can find a therapist who will give you a bulk rate.

Q.-9 Lately, our 17 year old daughter seems to spend most of her time in her room moping about some boy. What can we do to cheer her up?

A. Don't even try. If she is in her room moping about some boy, she is not out in the backseat of his car. Just leave her alone and hope the two of them don't make up anytime soon.

Q.-10 Now that our sons are in their teens, they are really too big for 'time outs' when they misbehave. What other methods of discipline are effective on teenage boys?

A. Wrapping all their limbs tightly with duct tape slows them down, but is very time consuming and can result in a nasty rash. The most effective way to discipline teenagers is to shut off their cash flow. However, caution must be used with this method because if they cannot go out, they will stay home and drive you right off the edge of a cliff.

Q.-11 During the increasingly frequent arguments between my daughter and myself, she often shouts, "I didn't ask to be born." Is there a good response to this?

A. Not really. None of us asked to be born. Just tell your daughter that her life could always be worse. She could have been born into the 16th century where there were no telephones, televisions or issues of "Young Glamorous Person" magazine.

Q.-12 I just don't understand the music my children listen to. What can I do?

A First of all, warm up your spaceship and prepare for the journey to the home world. You are not supposed to understand the music your children listen to. If you ever get even so much as a remote clue as to what their music is about, they will all get together and change it, which could be very bad. Remember the Bee Gees?

Q.-13 Since my son entered puberty, his personality has changed drastically. He used to go to church, mow the lawn and fold his own laundry, but lately he just sits on the couch, eats and watches inane network dramas with scantily-clad blond women in them.

A. You make that sound like a bad thing. Your son is becoming a man, and most men see absolutely nothing wrong with sitting on the couch, eating and watching inane network dramas with scantily-clad blond women in them.

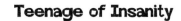 
Q.-14 Why are teenagers so belligerent and disrespectful to their parents?

A. Teenagers are belligerent and disrespectful to everyone. It is a form of cosmic justice, because they are being forced to endure puberty, driver's ed and bad skin all at the same time.

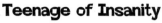 

Q.-15 Teenagers are not all bad. My 16 year old daughter is sweet, kind, thoughtful and attentive. She gets good grades, doesn't date and is always home by 10:00. Plus, she cleans her room and helps me with the ironing.

A. Yeah, so did Linda Blair before she found that Oujii board, and you know how that turned out. Look, kids as perfect as the one you just described exist only in the active imaginations of grandparents and very old Shirley Temple movies. Your daughter is simply up to something you haven't caught on to yet. Prepare for the worst.

Q.-16 How should parents react when their teenager questions them frankly about their own past experiences with drugs?

A Lie. And make it believable. Then change the subject. If necessary, give them money, and they will go away.

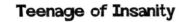 

Q.-17 My daughter says that most of her friends are already sexually active. I know she is very curious about sex, but how can I keep her from acting on her urges?

A. Encase her in cement up to her neck. If this does not dissuade the young men who show up on your doorstep every Friday night, simply make sure that you are engaged in some overtly protective act when your daughter's date arrives. Ostentatiously cleaning your shotgun is a good start, as is sharpening a large knife and glaring menacingly at young Romeo's private regions.

Q.-18 My spouse and I have saved a large sum of money for our oldest child, but now we are arguing about what Junior needs more: a good, dependable car or a year's college tuition. Which is more beneficial for a teenager?

A Neither. Junior can ride a bus to his job, flipping burgers for minimum wage, while he recycles soda pop cans for tuition money. You and your spouse should use the cash you've saved to take a nice cruise around the world. You'll need the time together, because as soon as Junior finishes college and sees what the job market is like, he'll move back home, and you'll have had a $25,000 lesson.

Q.-19 When my son turned 14, the family grocery bill practically doubled. I know that he is a growing boy and needs the additional food, but if he doesn't slow down, we'll be broke in a year. Can you suggest some inexpensive, healthy snacks?

A. There is no such thing as 'Children Chow' (an unfortunate oversight on the part of a certain pet food manufacturer). But in a pinch, those little plastic 'peanuts' used as a packing material will work just fine. Throw a little paprika on them, put them in a big bowl on the TV table and your teenager will never know the difference.

Q.-20 There is so much violence on television. How can I get my kids to read the Classics, instead of watching shows like "The Exterminator of Gory Death" and "Sensuous Serial Killers from San Fernando"?

A. The Classics? You mean like "The Iliad", where Achilles drags Hector's body around behind his chariot for several days? Or maybe "A Tale of Two Cities" where everybody gets beheaded and knits stuff? (and not necessarily in that order) Look, Mr. Egghead from the English Literature Department, if Willie Shakespeare was so enlightening and gifted, how come nobody has made a video game out of "MacBeth"?

Q.-21 It seems that lately our teenagers have stopped talking to us. How can we reopen the lines of communication?

A. Why? Just enjoy the silence. You've spent the last 10 years trying to get them to be quiet, and now that they are, you're fussing about it.

Q.-22 I don't think my 15 year old is mature enough to see most of the movies being produced today. How old should a child be when parents allow him to make their own viewing choices?

A I don't think my grandmother is mature enough to watch most of the movies being produced today. A child should be allowed to make his own viewing choices when he has at least two mortgages and either a receding hairline or an advancing waistline.

 **Teenage of Insanity**

Q.-23 Why do my teenage children have to listen to their music at such an elevated volume?

A Because they are so used to ignoring you that their ears don't work right anymore. They have to crank up the volume to get past the natural adolescent auditory barriers.

Q.-24 My husband and I want our daughter to go to college and are even willing to help with the expenses. However, she wants to take a year off to 'find herself.' What does she mean, and how can we put her back on the right track?

A Your daughter wants a year off because she is tired of getting up and doing things. Her quest to 'find herself' will probably be conducted mostly in her room (which, if she is anywhere near a normal kid, is probably messy enough to hide the body of Jimmy Hoffa) or at the mall, where she believes she will find herself with the aid of your credit cards. After you cut off her flow of cash and food and begin waking her up before noon, college will start looking pretty good.

Q.-25 We have three teenage sons and all they do is sleep.   We have tried to get them to get jobs, at least in the summer, but they are just not interested. How can we motivate them to work?

A. Stop feeding them. Remove the refrigerator, microwave and pantry from your kitchen and install vending machines. Then hide all your change. After a couple of days your sons will either get jobs or spend more time at the homes of friends whose parents haven't caught-on yet. Either way, they're out of your house, which is the whole goal of raising kids, anyway.

Teen Statistic

When exposed to the brilliant works of Albert Einstein, 9 out of 10 teenage girls will jeer with disdain and say something like, "So, he was real smart. But look at his hair."

Q.-26 Is it necessary to set a curfew for teenage kids?

A. Only if you want them to come home. A 16 year old without a curfew has no problem at all playing video games at an arcade until the blisters on his fingers prevent him from opening another bag of Cheez-Doodles. But a curfew will force him to come up for air about three hours after he was actually supposed to be home. It will also give him a chance to exercise his imagination, inventing creative excuses for not being home on time.

Q.-27 My wife says I worry too much when our 17 year old daughter is on a date. How can I learn to relax?

A You think you worry too much? About a hormone soaked, physically mature human female in the grips of a hormone dominated, adolescent male whose entire body is geared only to the reproductive process? Think back to what you were like as a teenage boy. Then lock your daughter in her room and guard the door. If your wife objects, remind her of what you two used to do at the drive-in when you were dating. She will probably end up relieving you on guard duty.

Q.-28 It seems like every day my kids need some new, expensive gadget or gizmo to keep them on the same level with their peers. I don't want them to be social outcasts, but this "keeping up with the adolescent Jones'" is putting a serious dent in our savings. When is it ok to say, "Enough"?

A. How did you manage to get even one kid into adolescence and still have some savings left? Your teenager's desire for new gadgets is the direct result of effective and pricey marketing by the gadget companies. It can only be avoided by planting petunias in the shattered remains of your television set and moving to a religious community that prohibits contact between people. This eliminates the rampant peer pressure, and will also give you some quality time alone.

Q.-29 My wife and I have seven children. The oldest is 16; the youngest is only 3. The oldest has developed a somewhat flippant, almost mocking attitude towards his mother and me, and we believe he is setting a bad example for the younger children. How can we stress respect to the oldest without seeming like control freaks to the younger kids?

A Control freaks? With seven kids?

Q.-30 We have set a time curfew on phone usage for our teenagers which they believe is unfair. They are not allowed to receive or make any phone calls after 10:00 pm. Is this a reasonable curfew?

A Absolutely. But you and your spouse are liable to become pretty unpopular in your own social circle, because you will always have to call your friends after 10:00 at night.

 **Teenage of Insanity**

Q.-31 My husband and I are going on a cruise around the world and will be gone for three weeks. Our 17 year old son insists that he is old enough to stay by himself, but my husband and I are not convinced. Should we trust our son alone for that length of time?

A An around the world cruise for three weeks? Wow, Mrs. Rockefeller, you want to know if you can trust a 17 year old male by himself in a house that he does not have to pay for, clean up or explain to the authorities? With your car in the garage and access to your checking account? Look, honey, when your ship cruises past Columbia, wake up and smell the coffee! If you've got money for a cruise, you've got money to hire a security guard. Not for your son, for your home.

Teen Myth

I'm a teenager, and I think…

Q.-32 When my son turned 16 I insisted he get a summer job at the local hardware store. The problem is that now we argue about his paycheck. I think he should put at least 40% in a savings account; he wants to spend it all. Who is right?

A. As always, the parent. The more money he saves now, the less you'll have to loan him later. But more importantly, can he get me a good price on a new cordless drill?

 **Teenage of Insanity**

Q.-33 Why do teenagers insist on such unusual hair styles?

A. For the same reason they insist on any other form of rebellion, like indecent clothing, loud rap music and skateboards: to annoy people. You see, when our kids are little, they are cute and everybody tells them so. But when they get bigger they are no longer cute, and they resent the loss of attention, so they attempt to recapture adult eyes by annoying them.

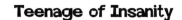 
Q.-34 What is it with these kids wearing their baseball caps backwards?

A. There are different theories about this mystifying practice. The most widely accepted one among adults is that today's teenager is not bright enough to figure out which way is forward. The drawback with this explanation is that some incredibly wealthy movie stars also wear their hats backwards, and they all have personal assistants who would get paid a great deal of cash to point out a social faux pas like a backwards hat. Another theory that has gained ground lately is that teenagers wearing their hats backwards are actually making a fashion statement, which if you think back to things like platform shoes and tie-dyed peasant shirts, is a distinct (though unpleasant) possibility.

Q.-35 Is there a good, effective way to dissuade a teenager from joining an unsavory crowd, without arousing their naturally rebellious streak?

A There is no way to do something as simple as saying 'Good Morning' to a teenager without arousing their naturally rebellious streak. When an adolescent joins an 'unsavory' crowd, your best bet is to purchase additional insurance and practice saying 'I told you so.'

Q.-36 Should you buy your teenager a car for her 16th birthday, or should you make her earn the money herself?

A If you make her earn her own money it will delay her vehicle ownership by years, which initially sounds like a good thing. Until you realize that she will be hounding you unmercifully for your wheels in the interim.

Q.-37 What have today's youth done to the English language? Instead of 'I said', it's 'It goes'. 'Yes, Sir' has become 'Yo, Dude' and 'I can do that' has disintegrated into 'No problemo'.

A. Ooooh, a wee bit self righteous, aren't we? Have you forgotten 'Groovy', 'Hep Cat' and 'Right On'? Did you just 'space out, Daddy-O', or are you blocking unpleasant memories? Personally, I much prefer 'Radical' over '23 Skidoo'.

Q.-38 Why don't kids today have any patience?

A Gee, I don't know. Could it have something to do with things like microwave ovens, fast food drive-thru windows and cellular phones? Teenagers did not create this society of instant gratification, we did. We shove a frozen pizza into the microwave, fast forward the video through the commercials and wonder why Junior can't wait.

Q.-39 How old should a teenage girl be before she is allowed to wear make-up?

A. Well, lets consider first why a teenage girl wants to wear makeup: to attract teenage boys, plain and simple. With that in mind, the logical answer is: a teenage girl should be allowed to wear make-up when she has reached her 32nd birthday.

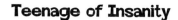 

Q.-40 My teenage son refuses to shave. His scraggly chin hairs look absolutely ridiculous and I am ashamed to take him golfing with me on Saturdays.

A. His scraggly chin hairs look absolutely ridiculous? But you have no qualms about putting on plaid britches that only reach your knees, a bright yellow polyester shirt, raspberry colored socks and a beret with a fuzzy pom pom on it and parading around with a golf club in your hand? Let's look up the word 'embarrassing', shall we, Doc?

Q.-41 Is there a way to make the experience of puberty any easier, not just for my teen, but for the entire family?

A. That's sort of like making the Black Plague a bit less fatal, isn't it? The only way to ease the experience of puberty is to send the pubert-or to live with Grandma for several years. This makes it easier for everybody except Grandma, but at her age she's just grateful for any visitors at all, so she's not likely to complain.

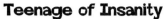 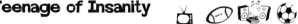
Q.-42 My son is on the football team, the track team and the debate team. He is also on student council and the yearbook staff. But lately his school work seems to be slipping well below average. Is there a way to improve his grades?

A You might try having him attend a class or two. With his extensive extracurricular schedule, it may be tough to find the time for actual schooling, but it's probably worth a shot. Yearbook staff and a letter in track sounds great in the annual family Christmas newsletter, but it makes for a very poor resume and does nothing for SAT scores.

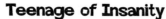 

Q.-43 Whenever we entertain guests our teenager disappears into her room. Why does she refuse to socialize?

A Maybe your guests are jerks. Actually, teenagers view all adults the way most people view extremely virulent diseases and avoid them at all costs. Your daughter is simply fulfilling a deep-seated desire not to talk to anyone except cute boys.

Q.-44 Speaking of cute boys, why do adolescent girls stare at any shirtless teenage boy they see walking down the street?

A. Because they have not yet learned what every grown woman knows, which is that if a guy is walking down the street without a shirt it is because he doesn't have a job, a car or enough money to buy decent clothes.

Q.-45 I am a single mother with a 15 year old son. Should I tell my son the facts of life or would it be better to have a male friend do it?

A Dip ever-so-briefly into the ozone of reality, dear. If he is 15, he could probably tell you some things about the facts of life. Today's kids learn that kind of stuff from the Saturday morning cartoons well before they are 10.

 **Teenage of Insanity**

Q.-46 It seems that when we were teenagers we were much more politically aware. Why don't today's kids show more interest in the political situations around them?

A Because no one has made a video game about it, and there are no exciting, well known political figures who make athletic shoe commercials as well as professional basketball players.

Q.-47 My daughter gets excellent grades, but is reluctant to admit it to her friends because she is afraid they would label her a 'geek'. How can I convince her that it is alright to be smart?

A. Get out your high school year book and show her the pictures of your school 'geeks'. Then, explain to her that most of them are now pulling down enormous salaries from major computer firms and flying first class at someone else's expense.

Q.-48 Whenever he is around his friends, my son treats me like a total idiot. Why is this, and can it be stopped?

A. Your son is suffering from the most heinous, crippling handicap a teenager can be afflicted with: parents. The only way he will even remotely tolerate your presence in public is if you pretend to be a member of his personal staff. (A low ranking member, at that.)

Q.-49 I was wondering if I should just let go and let my son handle his paper route by himself for a couple of days.

A As long as you remember that whatever he screws up today, you'll have to fix tomorrow.

Q.-50 Kids today don't listen.

A. So stop talking.

Q.-51 Doesn't it seem that this generation of adolescents has no respect for authority and structure?

A And whose fault might that be, Mr. Free-Love-and-Woodstock? 'Tune In, Turn On and Drop Out' was great for us, but it's not alright for our kids? Turn off your black light, roll up your fuzzy felt unicorn poster and grab a seat on the payback bus, 'cause you are about to reap what you and your electric purple bell bottoms sowed.

Q.-52 I'm fairly sure my 16 year old daughter has been sneaking out of the house through her bedroom window even though she is officially grounded. How can I be sure without making a groundless accusation?

A. Get a roll of that bubbly packing material. Spread it on the ground beneath your daughter's window. If you are awakened in the middle of the night by what sounds like a military takeover of a third world country, you'll know your daughter is being sneaky. You'll also know she'll probably need some clean pants, because you will have scared the you-know-what out of her.

Q.-53 Is it permissible for a girl to ask a boy out?

A. We are on the verge of a new and wonderful century and are witnessing the passage of many old-fashioned ideas, such as traditional gender roles and common courtesy. It is perfectly acceptable for a girl to ask a boy out. Of course, he still has to pay for everything.

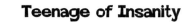 

Q.-54 I read about a teenage girl who sued a boy because he asked her to the school prom and then stood her up. What sort of lesson does this teach our youth?

A. That if you ask a girl to prom, you'd darn well better have a really good lawyer.

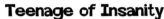 
Q.-55 Now that my kids are teenagers, is it a good idea to let them do their own clothes shopping?

A Is it a good idea to give your kids your credit cards and send them to the mall? Is it a good idea to give your dog the car keys? Your kids are perfectly capable of doing their own school shopping, as long as you don't mind their entire winter wardrobe consisting of two pairs of pre-torn jeans and a plaid miniskirt. (Of course, if they are male children, the plaid miniskirt will probably already have somebody in it.)

 **Teenage of Insanity**

Q.-56 Should high school kids be allowed to wear shorts to class?

A Only in Baja. Otherwise, the very last thing high school age kids need is more exposed flesh to distract their minds and hormones.

Q.-57 My son has a chance to participate in an exchange student program. He would be going to Germany for one year. He thinks it's a great opportunity, but we have some reservations.

A. I'd have some reservations, too. Namely on a fancy cruise ship. You have a chance to get rid of a teenager for a whole year, to make him someone else's problem entirely, in a place so far way that he will be unable to borrow money for weeks on end, and you haven't already packed his bags? Run, do not walk, to the airport.

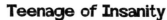 

Q.-58 How long do the moodiness and attitude problems of adolescence last?

A It begins to appear when the child turns 11 or 12. It seems to ease off once the child is in his or her early 20's and is being forced by life and weary parents to begin paying his own way. This is not encouraging, but it is fairly accurate. Scientists are working on a way to put pre-teens into a deep, cryogenic sleep until their 21st birthday. This should ease some of the stress, but will come too late for those of us already raising teenagers.

Q.-59 My daughter has invited her boyfriend for dinner, and she is terrified that her father and I will embarrass her. Can you suggest any guidelines for topics of conversation that will ease my daughter's worries?

A. Showing the naked baby pictures is always a good ice-breaker. Follow up with the stories about how your daughter wet herself at Aunt Sissy's wedding and put dried peas in her own ears. This is a fine test of character for the young man in question because if he stays with your daughter after an evening like that, he is of a serious mind.

Q.-60 Explain the 275 stuffed animals on my daughter's bed. She has to sleep on the floor because there is no room left.

A. Teenage girls are the ultimate cuddlers. This is why you see so many teenage couples liplocked in the mall. So, when a boyfriend isn't easily accessible, they cuddle inanimate objects. Care must be taken that the total stuffed animal weight does not overload the bed, however, because injuries incurred when 'Fluffy', 'Boodles' and 'Ziggy' fall on her are not covered by your insurance.

Q.-61 My daughter has been crying for three straight days. She's still eating, but has refused to speak coherently with either her mother or myself. All we can get out of her is, "You wouldn't understand" and, "My life is over." We are getting worried. What's up?

A. This sounds serious. It's highly possible that your daughter is in deep social trouble. Three days of weeping may indicate something serious, like she wore the same dress when she was a freshman or her boyfriend was seen talking to a cheerleader. All you can do is keep her in tissues and chocolate covered peanuts.

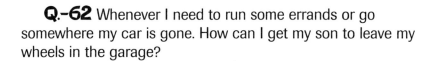

Q.-62 Whenever I need to run some errands or go somewhere my car is gone. How can I get my son to leave my wheels in the garage?

A Drain the tank. Your son will not take your car if it has no fuel. When you go to drive it, put just enough gas in it to get where you need to be.

Q.-63 There are four of us in my family. My wife and I, our 10 year old son and a 14 year old daughter. The problem we're having is that whenever the phone rings, it's always for my daughter. No one calls my wife and me anymore because they can never get through.

A Get used to it. And get a voice mail system that, when the line is busy, routes all incoming calls to leave a message. Then, when your daughter goes to school, you can return calls.

Q.-64 Why does my adolescent fight with his younger brothers and sisters so much?

A. They are the only ones in the house with whom he can win an argument, so he feels empowered. The only way to take the pressure off his younger siblings is to buy a small, helpless, stuffed animal for him to torture.

Q.-65 Our family has been planning a trip to Wisconsin for several months. Yesterday, our oldest child informed us that she doesn't want to go; she'd rather stay home. All the flight and hotel arrangements have already been made, and it is too late to cancel one of them. My concern is that if we force our daughter to go, she'll ruin the trip for the rest of us with her moping and whining.

A. Not if she's heavily sedated. A tranquilized teen is an agreeable teen, and those are the only kind who are any fun at all when you travel. She'll float right through those dairy farms with scarcely a murmur of discontent, and your entire family will enjoy the trip.

 **Teenage of Insanity**

Q.-66 My teenager would live on junk food if I'd let him. He loves pastries, chips, soda pop and burgers. I'm afraid this type of diet is going to cause him harm.

A. Look at it this way. If he continues eating like that, when he dies, the incredible level of preservatives in his blood will spare the need for embalming.

Q.-67 Do teenage boys think about anything but sex?

A. Yes. They also think about cars. Sometimes they think about having sex in cars, which saves them from further thinking for the rest of the day.

Q.-68 Lately, my husband and my son have begun rebuilding an old car. I think it's great that they're spending so much time together, but I feel left out. Is there something I can do as a woman to get involved?

A. Sure. Bring them lemonade and nachos from time to time. If it's winter, bring them coffee and chili.

Q.-69 My teenager does not have a job, yet lately I've noticed that she always has lots of money. When I ask her where she got it, the answer is always 'from a friend'. Do I have a reason to be concerned?

A Big time. Better make sure her 'friend' isn't a 68 year old man whose wallet is bigger than his moral character. If it turns out that she really does just have a wealthy girl companion, immediately make arrangements to befriend the girl's mother.

Q.-70 Is there a reason teenagers spend so much time in the bathroom?

A The length of time kids spend in the bathroom is directly proportional to the number of bathrooms you have in your house. So, if you only have one bathroom, your child will be in there forever. They do this on purpose because they are trying to help prevent 'empty nest' syndrome. When they finally move out you will be so glad to get the bathroom back you won't miss the kid for weeks.

Q.-71 Why does it seem that childhood is so brief but adolescence drags on forever?

A. Same reason a day off speeds by but a committee meeting is eternal.

Q.-72 My son recently obtained his driver's license. Now he wants to borrow my showroom-new, very expensive, incredibly fast, imported European sportscar. Should I let him?

A Absolutely. And then you should send me a check for a very large sum of money which I promise I will pay back soon. Really.

Q.-73 Is there a way to make an adolescent concentrate on her studies instead of her social life?

A No. If there were, the pages of "Young Cool Person" magazine would be filled with articles like 'Sliderules and You' and 'What to Wear for Those Late SAT's' instead of 'Should you Kiss and Tell?' and 'Hot Hunks of Prime Time'.

Q.-74 How can I tell if my teenager is doing drugs?

A. Any change from their normal behavior pattern is cause for concern, so if they are suddenly easy to get along with, friendly and affable, it's time to worry. If they begin hugging you spontaneously and cleaning their rooms, panic.

Teen Myth

Not all teens are moody and sullen.

Q.-75 My teenager is reluctant to help out around the house. Insisting only makes her sullen, but I believe kids should do household chores so that they will have adequate life skills when they move out. Is it a good idea?

A. Anytime you can get somebody else to do the ironing it's a good idea. If chores make her sullen, simply assign her chores in another part of the house so you don't have to watch her sulk.

Q.-76 It's time for that dreaded 'facts of life' talk. Is there an easy way to discuss these things?

A. No. Your best bet is to use lots of colorful euphemisms like 'Mr. Winkie' and 'you know' and 'that thingie'. Add a couple of 'ummms' and 'errrrs' and you will join the hoards of nervously uncomfortable parents who have already talked the talk.

Q.-77 My son is 17 and has no idea what he wants to do with his life. Should my spouse and I be worried?

A Look, some people who are well into their fifties have no idea what they want to do with their life. Some career politicians retire from office and still have no idea what they did with their life. As long as your son does not join a grunge rock band or shave a professional basketball player's name into his head, don't worry.

Q.-78 How can teenagers be encouraged to wear their safety belts when driving?

A Have a parent sit in the back seat of the car whenever the teenager is driving. This also cuts way down on unauthorized horsing around, and 'Wooo Baby' exclamations from members of the opposite sex. (Unless, of course, the parent in question is a real babe.)

Q.-79 Is it possible to involve teenagers in world affairs?

A Only if the affair has to do with an innovative acne medicine or new clothes. Also, it helps if the affair is very popular and doesn't involve getting up early.

Q.-80 How old should a teenage girl be before she is allowed to date?

A. This modern world has seen many changes and the old fashioned values are rapidly becoming outdated. With this in mind, the acceptable dating age for a girl should be moved up to 30 or at least 28. For a boy, 45+, but only if he's had all his shots.

Q.-81 Should a teenager be allowed to have her own private phone line?

A Only if you ever expect to use your own telephone. However, your bill will begin arriving in volumes, like an encyclopedia, and will reflect any long distance romances your child has going.

Q.-82 Since my son got his driver's license we have spent more money on car insurance than on mortgage payments. Why is the insurance so high for teenage male drivers?

A. Have you ever driven anywhere with your son? Teenage guys operate a motor vehicle like a logger runs a chainsaw; whatever is in the way is going down, and it will not be pretty. The insurance companies figure that if they place a heavy financial burden on the male youth of America, they will not have enough money left to fill their gas tanks and will have to stay off the roads.

Q.-83 The biggest event at my daughter's middle school is the annual Spring dance. Yet, even though the student council spends a great deal of money hiring a mobile DJ, only a few of the kids actually dance. Why?

A. Because although it is considered extremely 'cool' to attend a dance, it is the highest mark of geekiness to indulge in dancing. The proper behavior for a teenage dance-goer is to strike a pose that indicates extreme boredom while trying not to look at any member of the opposite sex.

Q.-84 Is it possible to keep a good mental attitude while raising teenagers?

A. Only with the liberal use of prescription medications.

Q.-85 How come some teenage boys are now wearing more earrings than their mothers?

A They have more money than their mothers ever did. Also, since they are guys, they only have to buy an earring for one ear, which saves them a great deal of cash.

Q.-86 It seems that today's teens have lost the art of reading. They are so bombarded with video games and violent television shows that they have forgotten how to entertain themselves.

A. Not really. After all, it must take a great deal of skill to read that cryptic graffiti that they scrawl all over road signs and buildings. Heaven knows adults can't make any sense of it.

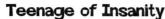 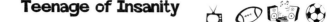

Q.-87 I know my daughter is bright, but her grades have dropped sharply since she started high school. She keeps telling me her teachers don't assign homework, and that is why I never see her studying. I have begun to doubt this.

A. I think it is fortunate for our space program that you don't work for them. It is a devastating career move for a high schooler to be seen carrying school books of any sort. This results in a need for 'stealth studying', which is doing school work without actually bringing books home. Your daughter has apparently not mastered this art yet. Rejoice in the fact that because she has learned the fine art of conformity, she is probably not a social outcast, and will have plenty of friends to borrow money from when she is unable to land a decent job.

Q.-88 My daughter recently made the cheerleading squad at her school...

A I'm sorry to hear that.

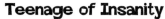 
Q.-89 Thanks, but I was hoping for some advice as to how to get her to stop flopping around the house like a gutted fish.

A. Well, question one suggests full body restraints, but that's obviously not practical all the time. Cheerleaders are packed to the gills with exuberance, and unless you can find a way to drain some of that off, you'll never get her to calm down. Try threatening to take away her contact lenses and make her wear horn-rimmed glasses. The thought of such an impending social catastrophe will probably put a damper on some of those big hand motions.

Q.-90 My teenage son seems to be obsessed with sports. I try to get him to concentrate on school, but he is only interested in making the varsity football team. I had such high hopes that he would be a doctor.

A. Doctors, if they are established and have been practicing for years, can come close to making the same amount of money as a rookie linebacker. They do not get commercial endorsements and are never asked to do sportscasting for major television networks. You figure it out.

Q.-91 Why does my teenager spend so much time in his room?

A So he doesn't have to talk to anyone. Teenagers believe that they are so superior to the rest of their family that it is beneath them to speak to someone.

Q.-92 I suspect that my kid has been sneaking a beer from time to time. How can I make the evils of alcohol clear to him?

A. Well, showing him the photos of you at the office Christmas party might do the trick.

Q.-93 For her sixteenth birthday, my husband and I gave my daughter a car. But when we found out that she had been using it to drive to the mall and cut classes, we suspended her driving privileges. Now she's accusing us of buying the car so that we'd have another means of control over her.

A. Nice job. If it works, go with it. 'The keys are mine' beats the yahoo out of 'you're grounded'.

Q.-94 My daughter is dating a boy who gives the appearance of being a reform school poster child. How can we get her to break up with him?

A. Approve of him in a loud, vocal, parental manner. Invite him to dinner and tell your daughter how wonderful you think he is. Within a week, she'll drop him like a bad habit.

Q.-95 My son has joined a garage rock band. The problem is we don't have a garage, and they are practicing in the basement. I want to encourage my son's musical interests and nurture his talent, but the noise is driving me right over the edge. What can I do?

A. Since the terms 'musical talent' and 'rock band' are generally mutually exclusive, your best bet is to move to a house with a garage. Just don't tell your son why you're moving.

Q.-96 What do today's teenagers do at rock concerts?

A. Today's teens are far more trendy than we ever were. They do not waste their time with mind altering substances, nor do they concern themselves with trying to get backstage to party with the band. Instead, they discuss current political events and circulate petitions to save the spotted owl. The biggest problem they face is where to park the trendy European sports car so that the bicycle rack won't get scratched.

Q.-97 My daughter has a curfew of 11:00 pm. Her boyfriend has always been aware of this, yet last Friday night he did not bring her home until well after 3 am. What in the world could they have been doing until that ungodly hour?

A. The same thing they were doing until 11:00 pm, only three more times.

Q.-98 Do teenagers still cruise down Main Street like we did in high school?

A Absolutely. Except we did it in a beat up orange Gremlin with no working taillights, and kids today are liable to be cruising in a car that cost more than our first house.

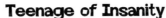 

Q.-99 My ex-husband and I share joint custody of our teenage daughter. He gets her two weekends a month and one month in the summer. The problem is that since my daughter entered adolescence, my ex seems to find an increasing number of excuses why he can't take our daughter for his scheduled weekends. I think he's just trying to get out of dealing with her during this difficult time.

A. You thought that out all by yourself? I am getting a sunburn from the brainwaves you are emitting. Tell your ex that if he doesn't hold up his end of the bargain, you will take him to court and demand that he take your daughter until she turns 21. He'll mellow out real fast.

Q.-100 Should teenagers be allowed to go co-ed camping without an armed escort?

A. Not even for 15 minutes. A co-ed camping trip requires more security, safeguards and firepower than an armored car on its way to the bank. Hiring mercenaries is not out of the question.

 **Teenage of Insanity**

Q.-101 Why does a teenager's room consistently look as if his closet has thrown up?

A. Teenagers are busily moving from childhood to adulthood. They do not have time for small things like cleaning and organization. Besides, teenagers see that the federal government will often set aside money for disaster areas, and teenagers never have enough money.

Q.-102 What is a mosh pit? My teenager seems to love it, but every time he has been to one, he comes home all bruised-up.

A. A mosh pit is this decade's equivalent of Woodstock. The mosh-ee, driven by large amounts of straight tequila and massive doses of power chords, throws himself into a group of rabid pit bulls, who quite naturally tear him to pieces. It's sort of like doing the Hustle, without the polyester clothing.

Q.-103 Why do teenagers take relationships so lightly? It seems like my daughter is always falling in love, breaking up or somewhere in between.

A. Well, since this is the decade of revolving door marriages and drive-thru divorces, I'd guess they get it from us. Most adults today get a bulk rate on divorces and buy enough wedding rice to feed a small Asian country. You figure it out.

 **Teenage of Insanity**

Q.-104 Why do teenagers assume they know it all and their parents know nothing?

A. Look at it from their point of view. Their parents wore bell bottoms, gold chains and white polyester. Kids today get to wear pants that are three sizes too big, backwards baseball hats and tennis shoes that light up. They are so much more sophisticated than their parents, it's not even funny.

Q.-105 How can I get my teenager to spend more time at home?

A. Install snack machines, two more televisions and another telephone. You won't get much quality time, but they will be home.

Q.-106 Whenever my kids need new clothes, they always pick the most expensive item they can find. Why can't they be a little less extravagant with my money?

A Two reasons. First, anything less than the most expensive item would drop them down several notches on the social scale. Second, teenagers are very good at spending somebody else's money. If they had to buy their own clothes, they would wear trash bags and old newspapers.

Q.-107 I can always tell when my teenager is home, because he goes through the house leaving a trail of discarded clothing, sort of like Hansel and Gretel with a laundry fixation. Why can't he pick up after himself?

A. He is physically unable to do so. The condition is called 'weak arm syndrome' and is caused by playing too many video games. This makes it impossible for your teenager to bend down and pick up dropped clothing. Your best bet is to buy a whole bunch of laundry baskets and line them up along your son's path of choice.

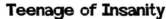 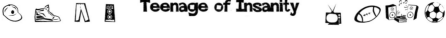

Q.-108 My daughter has decided to become a vegetarian and refuses to eat anything with animal products in it. My husband and I both work full-time and it is extremely inconvenient to fix two separate meals for one family. Any attempt to talk to her about her new dietary habits just results in a lecture about how cruel it is to eat animals.

A. Your daughter is just manifesting another symptom of the 'everything my parents do is stupid and thoughtless' disease that afflicts all kids between the ages of 13 and 21. If you and your husband were already vegetarians, your daughter would tell you that you were oversensitive tree-huggers. Tell her that you do not have time to accommodate her eccentric eating habits and that until she decides to fix her own meals, she will get lawn clippings on a plate for dinner.

Q.-109 How can I help my teenager decide where to go to college?

A. Look through all the college brochures carefully. Study the courses offered, the quality of instruction provided and the success ratios of past graduates. Then, look at the tuition and choose whichever one will still leave you with enough coins to jingle together.

Q.-110 My daughter did not get asked to her senior prom, even though she has a lovely personality and a sweet disposition. She is absolutely devastated and her mother and I are not having much luck in cheering her up. What can we do?

A. Not much. Sweet dispositions and lovely personalities are fine for blind dates and saddle horses, but when it comes to a prom date, teenage boys are looking for dangerously attractive girls with low cut formal gowns and non-existent curfews. Your daughter will only begin to cheer up when she realizes that she did not have to have one of those stupid pictures taken. Give her 30 years or so.

Q.-111 Even though he is only 11, my son is beginning to exhibit some of the rebellious, disrespectful attitudes normally associated with adolescence. Does this mean that his teenage years are going to be worse than normal?

A. It simply means he's getting a running start at driving you completely insane. The preteen years are formative for things like attitude, so your son is practicing his. Just remember that at age 11, he is still five years away from your car keys. That may be the only comfort you have.

Q.-112 When my son was in grade school he was a Cub Scout, and then a Boy Scout in junior high. However, now that he is in high school, he has dropped out of scouting all together. Why do you suppose he would abruptly lose interest in such a fine organization?

A. No question about it. That funky uniform. No normal high school boy wants to go through class dressed like a big green bean. And where's the fun in helping little old ladies across the street when there are cheerleader's books to be carried?

Q.-113 'Mom' I like. 'Ma' I can deal with and I can even tolerate 'Yo, Momma'. But 'Mother', with the sarcastic accent on the second syllable really hacks me off. Why does my daughter insist on making the word 'Mother' sound like a derogatory remark?

A. Because it really hacks you off. Your daughter is trying to tell you that she thinks you are an idiot, whose only purpose is to do her laundry and pay the phone bill. In her eyes, the only term more derogatory than 'Mother' is 'Teacher'. Don't worry too much. When she has children of her own, the word 'Mother' will gain a whole lot more respect.

Q.-114 At what age should a child be held responsible for his own actions?

A. If a two year old steps out of his britches and runs through the back yard, it is a humorous manifestation of youthful exuberance. If a 12 year old does the same thing, the county social worker will almost certainly be paying the parents a visit. So, when a child's actions cross that line between innocent amusement and bad taste, he should be held responsible for them. And grounded until he's 30.

Q.-115 My mom says I can't wear make-up until I'm 17. I don't think she's being fair. I think 14 is plenty old enough and besides, all my friends wear make-up to school.

A. The drive to wear make-up is an overwhelming urge, like popping those little plastic air bubbles on protective wrapping and checking the pay phone coin slot, even though you heard the quarter drop. The only way to overcome this urge is to look at a photo of that televangelist's wife when she was having a good cry. This proves that make-up does not necessarily make you attractive; it can make you look like you ran into a paint truck.

Q.-116 Why do I have to take history in school and learn about things that happened way before I was born?

A. There are those who say that we must learn from history, lest it repeat itself. Personally, I think we should learn about things that happened way before we were born so that we will be very grateful we didn't live back then. Check out the 1870's, for example. Teenagers in the 1870's were expected to work all day on their parent's farm, do household chores and go to bed early.

 **Teenage of Insanity**

Q.-117 Several times, I have asked my teenage daughter to baby-sit her younger brother. She always resists and tells me that she doesn't want to baby-sit because she has a life of her own. I only ask when I really need her to. What can I do to make her more agreeable to helping out?

A Remind her that while she does, indeed, have a life, you have given up most of yours to raise her. Use guilt, shame and reproach if you have to. If those don't work, remind her gently that the life she has rests precariously in your stressed-out hands.

 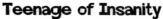 
Q.-118 My teenager sleeps very late on weekends. I believe he would sleep until sundown if I'd let him. Is it wrong to wake him up before he's ready?

A. Not only is it perfectly alright to wake up a sleeping teenager, but it can be a great deal of fun if done correctly. My suggestion is to place your stereo speakers near his bed and very loudly play the first part of the Pink Floyd song 'Time', the one where it starts out with all those alarm clocks going off at once. It is really amusing to see your child jump out of bed without bending his knees.

Q.-119 Whenever my daughter gets a facial blemish, she goes into an emotional tailspin, sometimes even refusing to go to school until her face clears up. I think she's putting too much emphasis on her appearance.

A. High school is a vicious world. The wrong color socks can send a social life into the gutter. A big blemish can completely ruin a person and will be talked about on the teen grapevine for weeks. Try and understand what your daughter is going through and offer to pick up her homework for her.

Parents of Teens Aptitude Test

Q.-120 What is the proper response to a teenager who wants to dye his hair a vibrant shade of blue?

A. "Over my dead body."
B. "Not while you live in this house, buster."
C. 24 hour-a-day supervision.

Answer: **(C)** If he's thinking about dying his hair blue, he should have had this type of supervision a long time ago.

 **Teenage of Insanity**

Q.-121 Sometimes when I come home from work my son has invited his friends over, and there is a group of unidentified teenagers in my house. They eat my food, trash my house and ruin the furniture. I want my son to be popular and well liked, but his generosity is wrecking my home.

A. Explain to your son that you are only going to buy so much junk food a week. When that is gone there will be no more for another week. Teenagers, like stray dogs, will not come back if you don't feed them. They will go find somebody else to bother.

Q.-122 Instead of going to college, my daughter wants to sell pottery in New Mexico. She wants to use her college fund to buy a kiln and a loft apartment. Is this a good idea?

A. Loft apartments are never a good idea. They lead to macrame wall hangings and subtitled foreign videos. Tell your daughter that since she doesn't need a college degree to sell pottery to New Mexican tourists, you are using the money earmarked for her education to take a cruise around the world. Don't worry, by the time you get back she will have fled the sunny climes of New Mexico to take shelter in her old room again.

Q.-123 Should a teenager be required to call home and check in with parents?

A. Always a good idea. If your adolescent doesn't let you know where he is and when he will be home, there is always the chance that he will make an untimely entrance, maybe even while you and your wife are having a nice, quiet dinner. If you still remember how.

 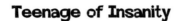 

Q.-124 My teenage daughter is very shy. She doesn't go out, doesn't run around the mall with her friends and doesn't date. What's wrong with her?

A. What's wrong with you? You've got a kid you can keep track of, don't have to worry about on a Friday night and don't have to mortgage your house to support. Don't ruin a good thing.

Q.-125 Is it legal to ground your teenager for periods longer than one decade?

A Yes. In some cases, such as 'crashing the car into a row of mailboxes' and 'staying out all night with boyfriend even though you had a 12:00 am curfew', the appropriate grounding period is in excess of 30 years. 'Getting caught with liquor in the car' carries a mandatory penalty of 375 years in your room, plus 100 straight years of 'taking out the trash.'

Q.-126 How many teenagers does it take to screw in a light bulb?

A. I don't know. You never said this was going to be on the final.

Q.-127 Why are so many teenagers wearing pagers now?

A. They are much more important than you were when you were a teenager. At least they think so.

Q.-128 How can I discourage my daughter from borrowing my clothes?

A Start wearing those stunning polyester ensembles found in the 'mature woman's sportswear' section of any major department store. Select pleasing colors like lime green and magenta. Two things will happen simultaneously: your friends will ostracize you completely, and your daughter will stay out of your closet.

Q.-129 Twenty minutes after eating a huge meal my teenage son is hungry again. What does is take to fill him up?

A Teenage boys are completely hollow. To make matters worse, the bottomless vat of hormonal stew they generate eats its way right through whatever you feed them, leaving them hungry as soon as they put down their fork. Invest in a truckload of bread, a vat of peanut butter and a bunch of paper plates. There's nothing else you can do.

Q.-130 Whenever I give my kid a ride anywhere, like to school, the mall or a friend's house, he insists that I let him out a block or so away so he isn't seen with me. Why?

A. Offhand, I'd guess it might be your 1974 lemon-yellow Gremlin with the dented left quarterpanel. If not that, your stunning, baby-blue housecoat and fuzzy bunny slippers could be the problem.

Q.-131 Kids today are always in a hurry to grow up. They never just take time to enjoy their life. Why can't they slow down?

A Because adulthood, with its mortgage payments, high blood pressure, 12 hour work days, insurance profiles and low fat diets, is stalking them relentlessly and they know it. Let 'em hurry now, while they have the energy.

Q.-132 I can't believe the way kids dress for school. We used to have a dress code when I was in school, but nowadays kids go to classes in shorts, mini-skirts and T-shirts with obscene messages scribbled on them.

A We had a dress code at our school, too. Girls couldn't wear pants, only skirts, and let's talk about how awkward that was on field day. But kids today feel it's necessary to express themselves through their clothing, which unfortunately includes lace up work boots with their mini-skirts and nasty messages on their T-shirts. Just be glad they're dressed and try not to read their shirts out loud.

Q.-133 One of my daughter's teen magazines refers to her age group as 'the angry generation'. What in the world have they got to be mad about?

A. They missed all the free love, free drugs and self-righteous protesting of the 60's. There is nothing left for them to gripe about that the older generation hasn't already griped about. It's no longer socially acceptable to do drugs, and free love nowadays will just get you killed. So they're pretty ticked-off as a generation.

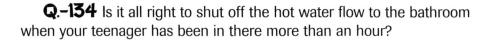

Q.-134 Is it all right to shut off the hot water flow to the bathroom when your teenager has been in there more than an hour?

A Perfectly acceptable. And very effective. This strategy will also help cut down on those multi-paged water heating bills. Just remember to turn it back on before you take your shower.

Q.-135 How can we help our 16 year old daughter deal with the acne that is inevitable with the onset of puberty?

A. Begin adhering to a strict Muslim lifestyle which will require her to wear a veil all the time. It couldn't hurt.

Q.-136 Are there any easy ways to get a teenager out of a video arcade?

A. Several. First, have the utility company cut all power to the arcade. If that doesn't work, try a tow chain wrapped tightly around the teenager-in-question's waist.

Q.-137 Every time my adolescent borrows my car she always reprograms all my preset radio stations. It drives me crazy.

A She knows that. To a teenager, radio stations are like outfits; they are another overt manifestation of her personality. She will continue to make your automobile airwaves her own as long as you let her drive your car. The only way around this is to remove the radio from your wheels and just whistle loudly whenever you drive.

Q.-138 Why do teenage girls giggle incessantly?

A. This constant giggling robs the brain of precious oxygen, necessary for all coherent thought processes, and thus prevents any intelligent neural relays from actually firing up. Just one more all-natural excuse for not doing homework.

Q.-139 Should teenage girls be allowed to read those torrid romance novels?

A. Why not? If they are reading torrid romance, they are not out doing it.

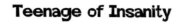 
Q.-140 Would you mind detailing the proper use of explosive devices for getting my son up off the sofa?

A. Not at all. The first thing to remember is that unless you knock out the power with the first explosion, he will not move. Make sure the amount of powder you are using is large enough to tip over a freight car with one shot and remember to cover the birdcage or face a truly gruesome clean up job.

Q.-141 Is it a good idea to hire a teenage baby-sitter or is a parent better off with an older sitter?

A. Better or cheaper? Teenage sitters are less expensive than older ones because older folks have more than likely raised kids of their own and know what to expect. They also know what it's worth on a financial level, to have someone tend your young children without dumping their squirming little bodies in a swamp.

However, older sitters rarely, if ever, get caught making out on the sofa. Weigh your options carefully before you choose.

Teen Myth

My son and I have a
paper route together.

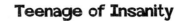 

Q.-142 It seems that teenagers learn about sex much earlier than we did. Is it really a good idea to educate them so thoroughly at such a young age?

A. Would you rather they picked it up (and heaven knows what else) in the backseat of a '57 Chevy, like most of your high school friends? Maybe by educating kids about the birds and the bees we can take some of the mystery out of it, and they can concentrate on getting a degree and a decent job.

Q.-143 Why are teenagers so involved with electronic equipment?

A. Because everything they deal with is computerized. Kids today aren't just computer literate, they're computer arrogant. They get faxes, pagers and voice mail, and that's just from their parents. This generation may someday rule the world, but if there is a power failure the planet is in deep doodoo.

Q.-144 Any tips on how to get a teenager to turn his 'garbage-truck-overturning-on-the-expressway' music down?

A In the event that threats of active physical violence don't work, swap his entire CD collection with the classic: "Music to Have Your Teeth Drilled By".

Q.-145 Why are my kids so weird?

A. Because you and your spouse were skinny dipping in the shallow end of the gene pool.

Q.-146 Should you argue with a teenager?

A Arguing with a teen is like eating ice cream with chopsticks. It can be done if you are careful, but it really doesn't prove much.

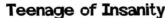  
Q.-147 My daughter says that it is tradition for the kids to get a hotel room for an after-prom party. Is it just me, or does this seem like a really bad move?

A. Bad on the scale of the Titanic's navigational plan. Drunken teenagers in formal wear do not belong in unsupervised hotel rooms. They belong in their own respective, individual beds, with the bedroom door locked from the outside.

Q.-148 Can the electronic tracking collars used by the people on those wild animal shows be utilized to track a teenager who has snuck out of the house to attend a forbidden party?

A Of course, and congratulations on your original thinking. By the way, just for reference, if you use the tranquilizer rifle as well, the dosage for a partying teen is about the same as a full grown male brown bear.

Q.-149 We punish our teen by sending her to her room, but this doesn't seem to bother her too much.

A 'Go to your room' loses something when the room is equipped with a phone, TV, fax, personal computer and snack bar. Sending a kid to a room like that is like punishing a glutton by forcing him to clean his plate. You have to be more ruthless, like forbidding her to view "Beverly Hills 90210" or making her wear loafers.

Q.-150 Should a teenager be expected to help pay for his class ring?

A Yes, because he will more than likely pawn it two years out of school in order to finance a really wild party.

Q.-151 What is the term for when a teenager says 'There's nothing to do'?

A We call that a 'mitigating circumstance', and any jury in the country will see it as grounds for acquittal in your murder trial.

Teen Fact

When my son says 'Mom, I love you' and 'Mom, you're the greatest', he always follows it with a request for something.

Q.-152 With this 'body piercing' craze sweeping the country, where should a parent draw the line?

A With their own kid. If human beings were meant to have holes in their navels, noses, tongues, lips, personal body parts that their swim suit covers or anywhere else, they would be born that way. Just say 'no'.

Q.-153 Why does my daughter spend hours on the phone with the same kids she spent all day with at school? Does that much really happen between the last bell and last call for supper?

A. The more they talk on the phone in the evening, the less they're (hopefully) doing it during school.

Q.-154 Teenagers think they know everything and are not in the least shy about telling anyone what they think.

A. That's because teenagers are like broken television sets. The volume is all the way up, but the brightness is inoperative.

Q.-155 Sometimes I get so tired of fighting with my teenage son that I just want to give up and let him go his own way.

A That is his strategy. He knows that if he wears you down enough, you'll break and he'll have his way. Remember, raising adolescents is the greatest battle you'll ever fight. Whatever you do, don't show the slightest bit of uncertainty. They're like wild dogs, they can detect the scent of fear miles away. Stay strong, and don't waver.

Q.-156 Why do adolescents delight in embarrassing their parents in public?

A. They are holding grudges for the little corduroy jumpers with the choo choos on them and the white frilly booties you put on them when they were too young to fight back. Each time a teenager embarrasses you in public, he is remembering one of the 'sit on Santa's lap and have your picture taken' episodes of his early childhood. Pray he never recalls the 'naked in the bathtub' thing.

About the Author Sherrie Weaver

The old saying about the pen being mightier than the sword is not necessarily true for Sherrie! Sherrie's writing has appeared in Comic Relief magazine and in Frank and Ernest cartoons.

Sherrie is the author of four published calendars:

The Dog Ate My Car Keys (And Other Great Excuses Not To Go To Work), the excuse-a-day calendar.

365 Days of Life in the Stress Lane, laughs to help you lower your blood pressure from someone who knows all about stress.

365 Reasons to Eat Chocolate, the sinful calendar with creative ways to indulge in chocolate every day.

How to Speak Fluent Child, the daily guide for parents to finally learn what their kids are saying.

as well as her paperback books:

The Secret Language of Men, a humorous look at what men say…versus what they mean and The Secret Language of Women, with the flip side explained for the benefit of men.

OTHER TITLES BY GREAT QUOTATIONS

201 Best Things Ever Said
A Lifetime of Love
A Light Heart Lives Long
A Teacher Is Better Than Two Books
The ABC's of Parenting
As A Cat Thinketh
The Best of Friends
The Birthday Astrologer
Cheatnotes On Life
Chicken Soup
Don't Deliberate . . . Litigate
Fantastic Father, Dependable Dad
For Mother–A Bouquet of Sentiments
Global Wisdom
Golden Years, Golden Words
Growing Up In TOYLAND
Happiness Is Found Along The Way
Heal The World
Hollywords
Hooked on Golf
I'm Not Over The Hill
In Celebration of Women
Inspirations

Interior Design For Idiots
Let's Talk Decorating
Life's Simple Pleasures
Money For Nothing, Tips For Free
Motivating Quotes For Motivated People
Mrs. Aesop's Fables
Mrs. Murphy's Laws
Mrs. Webster's Dictionary
Mrs. Webster's Guide To Business
Parenting 101
Real Estate Agents and Their
   Dirty Little Tricks
Reflections
Romantic Rhapsody
The Secret Language of Men
The Secret Language of Women
The Sports Page
Some Things Never Change
TeenAge Of Insanity
Thanks From The Heart
Things You'll Learn, If You Live
   Long Enough
Women On Men

GREAT QUOTATIONS PUBLISHING COMPANY
1967 Quincy Court
Glendale Heights, IL 60139-2045
Phone (708) 582-2800
Fax (708) 582-2813